PROCEDURAL ELEGIES
/ WESTERN CIV CONT'D /

PROCEDURAL ELEGIES
/ WESTERN CIV CONT'D /

Joan Retallack

Roof Books
New York

Cover art by Nick Keys.

ACKNOWLEDGMENTS
Existence Is An Attribute, *Dog City 2,* 1980; *New Directions 43,* 1981; (*How To Do Things With Words,* 1998). Earth Heaven and Hell, *The Little Magazine* 13, 1981; (*Circumstantial Evidence,* 1985). Oh Mother Goose Oh Yin Oh Yang, *Epoch* xxvii, no.1, 1978; (*Circumstantial Evidence,* 1985). The Problem of Evil, *African Golfer* 3, 1982; (*Circumstantial Evidence,* 1985). The Study of Time, (*Circumstantial Evidence,* 1985). A I D /I/ S A P P E A R A N C E, *Object* 5, 1995; (*How To Do Things With Words,* 1998). THE BLUE STARES, *CHAIN* 4, 1997. Not A Cage, (*How To Do Things With Words,* 1998). Steinzas In Mediation I-VII, (*How To Do Things With Words,* 1998). Witt & Stein, *Chicago Review* 49, no.2, 2003. Archimedes' New Light, *Conjunctions* 50, 2008. Lost Briefcase Conjecture, *POM 2,* 2002. Coimbra Poem of Poetry and Violence : Grief's Rubies (with Forrest Gander), *NO* 7, 2008. WESTERN CIV CONT'D, *Aerial* 4, 1988; *ABACUS* 49, 1989. N PLUS ZERO, *Ecopoetics* 6/7, 2009. PLUS A-Z, *PRESSED WAFER,* 2004; *Ecopoetics* 6/7, 2009.

Thanks To Qwerty
&
All The Rest

 This book is made possible, in part, by the New York State Council on the Arts with the support of the Office of the Governor and the New York State Legislature.

Roof Books are distributed by
Small Press Distribution
1341 Seventh Street
Berkeley, CA. 94710-1403
Phone orders: 800-869-7553
www.spdbooks.org

Roof Books are published by
Segue Foundation
300 Bowery
New York, NY 10012
seguefoundation.com

CONTENTS

This book contains selected work from the seventies to-date.

Procedure. The action or fact of proceeding or issuing from a source.
A methodical way of determining how to begin, how to go on, and some-
times—antecedent to elegy—how to end. 1695 E. POLHILL *Divine Will
Considered* (ed. 2) ix. 376 Those acts, which are above nature *in facto esse*,
as to their essential excellency, must be below it *in fieri*, as to their
procedure from causes.

Elegy. Specific gravity, specific humor: Song of lamentation as a tree that
is ouer plauntide vp on watris, that at the humour sendith his rootes.

Humor, Humour. Specific levity, conceptual fluidity; elegiac cast:
The skie hangs full of humour and I thinke we shall haue raine.
Thy strings mine elegy shall thrill, and too the organ of the humour of his
voluptuous melancholy.

now Jennie
has everything
she performs
every day and
twice on Saturday
she is content as
the archeology of our
thought easily shows
man is an invention
of recent date
and one perhaps
nearing its end
on this basis
modern positivism
erected a pure
methodology
purged however
of the really
interesting
problems
emptiness first
registered the
vibration that now
charms and
comforts and
helps?
I have thought
that the bird
makes
the same noise
differently

Sendak
Habermas
Foucault
Rilke
Stein

EXISTENCE IS AN ATTRIBUTE

> My answer is as follows. There is already a contradiction
> in introducing the concept of existence—no matter under
> what title it may be disguised—into the concept of a
> thing which we profess to be thinking solely in reference
> to its possibility....This is a warning against arguing directly
> from the logical possibility of concepts to the real possibility
> of things.   I. Kant, *Critique of Pure Reason*

A.

1. All I can remember is I thought I heard
2. jowls of the madonna on the car radio.
3. We had just passed the sign that says Darnestown.
4. There was a red, white and blue mailbox on the left
5. that said Owens. There was a cardboard box
6. in the middle of the road. It was raining.
7. You said, I can prove you don't exist:
8. If you exist, I can't prove you don't exist.
9. Either you exist or I am proving
10. you don't exist.
11. I am proving you don't exist.
12. You don't exist.

B.

1. All I can remember is I thought I heard
2. jowls of the madonna on the car radio.
3. as we passed the sign that says Darnestown, 8 mi.
4. I knew it couldn't be right, jowls.
5. You said you were going to prove I didn't exist.
6. This is no idle threat, you said, laughing.
7. Logic forces you to certain conclusions.
8. It was raining hard, mud washing onto the road.
9. All I can remember is "jowls" though I knew
10. only a split second later it couldn't be right.
11. You swerved to avoid what turned out to be
12. a box in the middle of the road.

C.

1-A. All I can remember is I thought I heard
1-B. All I can remember is I thought I heard

2-A. jowls of the madonna on the car radio.
2-B. jowls of the madonna on the car radio.

3-A. We had just passed the sign that says Darnestown.
3-B. as we passed the sign that says Darnestown, 8 mi.

4-A. There was a red, white and blue mailbox on the left
4-B. I knew it couldn't be right, jowls.

5-A. that said Owens. There was a cardboard box
5-B. You said you were going to prove I didn't exist.

6-A. in the middle of the road. It was raining.
6-B. This is no idle threat, you said, laughing.

7-A. You said, I can prove you don't exist:
7-B. Logic forces you to certain conclusions.

8-A. If you exist, I can't prove you don't exist.
8-B. It was raining hard, mud washing onto the road.

9-A. Either you exist or I am proving
9-B. All I can remember is "jowls," though I knew

10-A. you don't exist.
10-B. only a split second later it couldn't be right.

11-A. I am proving you don't exist.
11-B. You swerved to avoid what turned out to be

12-A. You don't exist.
12-B. a box in the middle of the road.

To carry on, set A, B, C....Z, 1-12 in any recombinations that include all
elements of A & B.

EARTH   HEAVEN   AND   HELL

there have always been reasons to pause
how now Ophelia what's the matter?
letting what was said sink in

O American Girl   Jack & Jill   Sport

begin at the end in the middle begin again
again the sentimental journey
flattened by gravity   emphasizing the point

O Better Homes & Gardens   The Runner   Ski

or stuffed with bachelor toast
here a brief moment due to scribal error
no doubt lost return lost again maybe

O Humpty-Dumpty   Road & Track   Rolling Stone

shriek laugh yell whistle scream bark
awaken in some basic human situation
sitting in a hole

O Modern Photo   Cuisine   Canoe

balancing on a wire   straddling an abyss
good old Attic tragedy   a handful of teeth
some fragments of jaw and a palate

O New Republic   Volleyball   Oui

high enough to disperse the smarting of the echo
come go with me to seek the Queen
we are in a foul mispickle

O Organic Gardening   Fantasy & Science Fiction   Vogue

besieged by the garlic-breathed muse
in the depured air and cruddy firmament
an unconscionably long dream-allegory

O Learning   Pick-Up Van & 4WD   Opera News

knowing glance into the absolute null
one must show one's hand with a heavy hand
hand to mouth thereby proving

O Car & Driver   Skin Diver   Stereo Review

existence of external world
uneducated as a waitress a working man a wave
lying on an inclined plane

O Mother Jones   Weight Watchers   Village Voice

saying even more asinine things
like the only edible integer is 13
the hypotenuse is a carnivore

O Bow & Arrow   Motorboating   Motor Trend

or reading How Grand Amour walked
in a Meadow and Met with Fame
Environed with Tongues of Fire

O Success Unlimited   Heavy Metal   Road & Track

April is the cruelest month, etc.
obiter dictum   as father used to say
optimism is a bourgeois invention

O Black Collegian   Outdoor Life   Ms.

where are the crisp sounds of everyday life
if the world ends next week
we will no longer be prophetic

O Family Handyman   Antique Monthly   Field & Stream

on razor thin nights a black brim
widens the sky   a welcome relief
pastimes of pleasure and pain

O Saturday Review   New West   Money

knees knocking like Hamlet's of course
scrabbling on the floor with Lear
flying into the eye with Amelia Earhart

O Black Enterprise   The Runner   Sea

nobody wants to forget or to be forgotten
flattened by gravity
then stuffed with bachelor toast

O Theater Crafts   Stock Market   Look

the broken clouds are pale as your face
you poor anonymous fool
your face is pale as your shirt

O Ladies Home Journal   Teacher   Prevention

shriek laugh yell shout whistle scream bark
fathoms bent and shining
pillars   pillars   pillars

O Popular Mechanics   Popular Electronics   Popular Photography

not so sour rhapsody
dear friends I address you
seeing you seldom or less

O High Fidelity   Redbook   New York Magazine

to transfix (meat) with a spit
to broach terrible subjects
with cosmetic beards

O Atlantic Monthly   Archery World   Cue

OH MOTHER GOOSE OH YIN OH YANG

In 1937 Professor Allen Abbott urged nursery rhyme reform, as did
Geoffrey Hall in 1949-50. And in 1952 Geoffrey Handley-Taylor of
Manchester England published a brief biography of the literature of
nursery rhyme reform in which he wrote:

> The average collection of 200 traditional nursery rhymes
> contains approximately 100 rhymes which personify all that is
> glorious and ideal for the child. Unfortunately, the remaining
> 100 rhymes harbour unsavoury elements. The incidents listed
> below occur in the average collection and may be accepted as
> a reasonably conservative estimate based on a general survey
> of this type of literature.

The Annotated Mother Goose

The man who knocks on my door says he's spreading
good news. Inside a ruined civilization
only 300 good deeds can make a saint
(8 allusions to murder, unclassified)
as the flea rides the rat rides the two-backed beast
it's the middle ages. I don't have the time.
I am trying to reclaim a cucumber tree
(2 cases of choking to death)
through the rictus of a very small opening.
Like Héloïse and Abélard
my methods must be indirect.
(1 case of death by devouring)
In the new world, looking for you in the crowd
I know that Venus Reproducing is a pencil
that Underwriter's Laboratory is the key
(1 case of cutting a human being in half)
to not short-circuiting the electric blanket.
This time the burglar lets us sleep.
The bear is stuffed with honey and cannot move.
(1 case of decapitation)
She takes the opportunity to write
the lightning bolt pilots all things
yes it comes in slips and snatches.
(1 case of death by squeezing)
She is not attempting to assemble a résumé.
She is not attempting to seduce the arid beast.
This is the story of the woman mad about honey
(1 case of death by shriveling)
her base seducer and her timid husband
how she wronged them all. No, how they
let her down. No, how it was no one's fault
(1 case of death by starvation)
how they all foundered in the cool shallows unaware
of the burglar making off with the stereo and jewels
running through the woods with the TV set
(1 case of boiling to death)
playing king of the mountain wearing her husband's
cowboy hat. Round about the maggoty pie
my father loves good ale and so do I.

(1 case of death by hanging)
Another cloistered moment hits the big time
from mythology to science her husband
the honey gatherer together with the sex therapist
(1 case of death by drowning)
turns up in a raid on a porno flick.
This is the cool side of the house. It takes
two weeks to train a flea and then you've got
(4 cases of killing domestic animals)
48 hours to get the show on the road.
I look for you in the crowd
yes I want that oceanic feeling
(1 case of body snatching)
Shakespeare's pulsing iambs the sweet bilge
of pregnancy. I am assembling a life.
The man who knocks on my door says he's chasing
(21 cases of death, unclassified)
the wild man out of the bush the wild man dies.
A stream of blood reddens the ground.
Without brutality they disregard
(7 cases relating to the severing of limbs)
the arid beast camouflaged in a dry season.
The man who knocks on my door has good news
the trail of honey never ends.
(1 case of the desire to have a limb severed)
Upstairs she screams she won't be blackmailed anymore
I know her only by her voice you can't hear his.
The carolers cover the building in the elevator
(2 cases of self-inflicted injury)
what has become of the promising young honey gatherer?
This time the burglar lets us sleep.
Is he the man knocking on my door selling
(4 cases relating to the breaking of limbs)
the Book of Knowledge? The feral boy is cooling
himself in the rain inside MILK is chalked
on the board the feral boy is eating
(1 allusion to a bleeding heart)
a piece of chalk. Your narrow snouted hound
has fleas. Sylvia shows the stigmata from

her honey bees where is her honey gatherer
(1 case of devouring human flesh)
going in that frayed mackintosh?
And where are the others the others?
Well they found her husband's cowboy hat
(5 threats of death)
floating in the river they found ashes
in the cornflakes fingerprints on the sill
they found the feral boy dead in a pile of leaves.
(1 case of kidnapping)
The wild ones shout the names of their dead in the forest
until their voices are bored into their chests
and names hang like kites from every tree.
(12 cases of torment and cruelty to human beings and animals)
She writes Dear Mom last night the burglar finally
let us sleep thank God we really need the rest.
Interspersed with eucalyptus leaves and ferns
(8 cases of whipping and lashing)
the lake is pulling pulling under the cold
splintered bone of the wind his cowboy hat
floats on top. I've got to start over now
(3 illusions to blood)
she says who's afraid of the undertow.
Orangutans hurl broken limbs at the visiting
scientists then fling themselves to the forest floor
(15 allusions to maimed human beings and animals)
die in fetal position. Back home
the scientist dies in fetal position
dreaming of the dance of the bees.
(14 cases of stealing and general dishonesty)
The young man's honey colored hair is trailing
from under his Panama hat did you know
they weave Panama hats under water
(1 allusion to undertakers)
he asks as they stare at him in silence
he is bleeding from the head
he can't find the words to flatten their faces
(2 allusions to graves)
a stream of blood reddens the carpet

the sound of their laughter comes from far away
Panama where Panama hats dry in the sun.
(23 cases of physical violence, unclassified)
Now it's time to gather your own honey babe
honeydew melon fruit of the moon
the lake is red as the harvest moon.
(1 case of lunacy)
Sorry we don't remember his name
door closes attendant checks lock
the nearest galaxies are in my spit he says
(16 allusions to misery and sorrow)
the man who opens my door is bringing
calming juices mixed with honey
oh yes yes please fix this head.
(1 case of drunkenness)
The arid beast is hiding in my breast
this time the burglar won't let me sleep
this time the burglar touched my thigh
(4 cases of cursing)
burning alive like his grandpa's tobacco
he never had a grandpa except in a picture
all those people are entering your room
(1 allusion to marriage as a form of death)
they find each other in the dark by body heat
in the house where she dropped her key
right into your smile three stories below.
(1 case of scorning the blind)
Decided to commit suicide last night
got drunk in order to commit suicide
got too drunk to commit suicide.
(1 case of scorning prayer)
Child's poem: my mother is a lovely woman
she doesn't stink up the room
she doesn't have a pimple on her nose
(9 cases of children being lost or abandoned)
she doesn't have sores between her toes.
What you need is a unifying vision
seeing at that moment of being lost
(2 cases of house burning)

that you are here lost here here not lost here
eating the fruit of the moon for breakfast counting
vitamins and minerals tuning and lubing the bowels
(9 allusions to poverty and want)
believe me the burglar is more afraid of you.
Men must hunt the wild boar before the sun.
If we sing not loud nor long what does it matter.
(5 allusions to quarreling)
Deafened by Brünnhilde's shouts the wolf
is creeping up in his underwear he is shot
the sheep may safely graze blood reddens
(2 cases of unlawful imprisonment)
his cowboy hat the man who knocks on my door
knows Latin like a scholar but not when he's
asleep "cucumber tree" is a misnomer
(2 cases of racial discrimination)
the arid beast is drinking milk and honey
and getting fat Ha! that'll do 'em in
the burglar is doing his best to let you sleep.

Expressions of fear, weeping, moans of anguish,
biting, pain, and evidence of supreme selfishness
may be found on almost every other page. G. H-T.

THE PROBLEM OF EVIL

1.

this is a game where the players have forgotten
the rules
no use telling sleeping dog lies
as you move about the blazing green and white grid
trying to look purposeful occasionally hopping
to keep from burning up
a Miss Pasta
has left another ominous message on the machine
in your empty apartment

yes truth is a strange experimental fiction
something for which the past has left you
unprepared like the figure who appears
in your dark bedroom and sneezes
before he puts his hand over your mouth

the fans are screaming
high above the lights
a blimp flashes
a message we can't make out
we are dazed
from the glare of the lights but
this is all beginning to sound highly metaphysical
and suspect
like a god dividing Light from Dark
or the Light of Reason
or Light at the End of the Tunnel
you are the light of my life he whispers

2.

this is a game where the players have forgotten
yes truth is a strange experimental fiction
the rules
something for which the past has left you
no use telling sleeping dog lies
unprepared like the figure who appears
as you move about the blazing green and white grid
in your dark bedroom and sneezes
trying to look purposeful   occasionally hopping
before he puts his hand over your mouth
to keep from burning up
the fans are screaming
a Miss Pasta
high above the lights
has left another ominous message on the machine
a blimp flashes
in your empty apartment
yes truth is a strange experimental fiction
a message we can't make out
something for which the past has left you
we are dazed
unprepared like the figure who appears
from the glare of the lights but
in your dark bedroom and sneezes
this is all beginning to sound highly metaphysical
before he puts his hand over you mouth
and suspect
the fans are screaming
like a god dividing Light from Dark
high above the lights
or the Light of Reason
a blimp flashes
or the Light at the End of the Tunnel
a message we can't make out
you are the light of my life he whispers

THE STUDY OF TIME*

> We are essentially rational but
> only accidentally earth-dwelling.
> Or is it the other way around?

this is part one we will
baptize this time by calling it
Sweet William in simple expiation
of verbal crimes Pound shut up
thank god at last Homeric men
weep more than Swedes and Englishmen
this is the fable of the box
or the miracle of cough syrup or both
the work of the dead is not done
nor the grammar of the last re-
corded announcement yes this is
it folks coeur de rigueur continu-
ing education fancy's class act

this is part two we will
baptize this time by calling it
the scholar's bookshelf bell peppers
plagiarize above the Loire too many
virgins of pastoral sucked to a
death 6,000 feet below it hangs
as an eggplant from the mast a
leitmotif or sign of typographical error
that is the periodic motion of the
sea &/or we have a kind of super-
ficial blandness that runs deep
ah yes to let the surface ripen
around a cool endogenous core

*to be read at an accelerating rate

this is part three we will
baptize this time by calling it
second rate song and dance it was
headlights perforate the air
another supermarket sunset breaks
sound barrier and tooth alike
ah the escapade of will seven-
teenth century your forte creased
and folded as were the sheets
in simple terms we come hi we go
bye mostly non-athletic modalities
if p is true so is possibly p even
the mirage may not be hallucinatory

this is part four we will
baptize this time by calling it
once again you are a living clock it's
half past seven time to affect that
pisiform excellence an alibi a seed
rationalist epiphany Hermes god of
hermeneutics in the Paris of the
Amazon rubber baron always gets
rubber maid in the end hi bye ex-
plosion of jargon quantum theology
blah blah I like sol better than gel
Keats is to Shelley as feets is to belly
pintle to gudgeon as the price of life

A I D /I/ S A P P E A R A N C E

for Stefan Fitterman

for Stefan Fitterman

1. in contrast with the demand of continuity in the customary description
2. of nature the indivisibility of the quantum of action requires an essential
3. element of discontinuity especially apparent through the discussion of the
4. nature of light she said it's so odd to be dying and laughed still it's early
5. late the beauty of nature as the moon waxes turns to terror when it wanes
6. or during eclipse or when changing seasons change making certain things
7. disappear and there is no place to stand on and strangely we're glad

A I D S
for tefn Fttermn

1. n contrt wth the emn of contnuty n the cutomry ecrpton
2. of nture the nvblty of the quntum of cton requre n eentl
3. element of contnuty epeclly pprent through the cuon of the
4. nture of lght he t o o t be yng n lughe tll t erly
5. lte the beuty of nture the moon wxe turn to terror when t wne
6. or urng eclpe or when chngng eon chnge mkng certn thng
7. pper n there no plce to tn on n trngely we're gl

B H J C E R T

fo fn Fmn

1. n on w mn of onnuy n uomy pon
2. of nu nvly of qunum of on qu n nl
3. lmn of onnuy plly ppn oug uon of
4. nu of lg o o yng n lug ll ly
5. l uy of nu moon wx un o o wn wn
6. o ung lp o wn ngng on ng mkng n ng
7. pp n no pl o n on n ngly w gl

F G K Q U

o n mn

1. no n w m no on ny no my pon
2. o n nvly o nm o on n nl
3. lm no onny plly pp no on o
4. no l o o yn nl ll ly
5. l y o n moon wx no own wn
6. o n l pow n n no n n mn n n
7. pp n no pl o no n n nly w l

L P V

o n mn

1. no n w m no on ny no my on
2. o n ny o nm o on n n
3. m no onny y no on o
4. no o o y n n y
5. y o n moon wx no own wn
6. o now n n no n n mn n n
7. n no o no n n n y w

M O W

n

1. n n n n n y n y n
2. n n y n n n n
3. n n n y y n n
4. n y n n y
5. y n n x n n n
6. n n n n n n n n
7. n n n n n n y

N X

1. y y
2. y
3. y y
4. y y
5. y
6.
7. y

Y

1.
2.
3.
4.
5.
6.
7.

THE BLUE STARES

Written On Barbara Guest's Blue Stairs

André Broca's Paradox: *To see a blue light,*
you must not look directly at it.
                    Julia Kristeva, "Giotto's Joy"

THE first color

to appear
twilight BLUE
having reached the summit
at start of day si sentono STARES
then begins again the THE *would like to stay*
detached BLUE not identifying the ob ab ject sche
STARES into blue noir space of THE *even if the stairs*
are the very BLUE sunrise Malev drew dotted lines *withdrawn*

There is

no fear Malev THE there kijárat (exit) the BLUE opt (now)
thesis under your seat STARES there in no THE *in taking the*
first BLUE *step* Malev *or the second or* STARES *the third* in
THE fact kijárat (exit) Malev BLUE *having a position between*
several Popes STARES when sche assumpte THE *in fact the*
top BLUE a life's work rendered entirely obsolete STARES az
ülés alatt THE *can be reached* Malev BLUE taking in the *with-*
out disaster precocious STARES dark middle row THE *the*
code in noticing BLUE

the particular shade occasionally giving way STARES isn't it cold THE hot today milyen ma! BLUE find an argument *of the staircase* STARES the question of the THE now Malev *occasionally giving* BLUE *way to the emotions* supporting assertions STARES *it has been* THE *chosen   discriminately* sche said BLUE *to graduate the dimensions* Malev plagiarizing STARES the fear of THE *ease them into sight* BLUE palace of culture concrete grey Danube STARES in the small of THE *republic of space* in the BLUE of in the Budapest apartment in the of of the musicologist's silence STARES *radiant*

everything a THE a republic of space BLUE tudja mit akar igen nem probleme STARES deepnest everything a THE *a thumb* pieta perforating BLUE Tuscan martyrs in the Museum's cold STARES saints wince under cleavers THE generácio opt (now) *passed* BLUE *over it disarming* the pocked blue STARES now everything a THE a thumb a pieta BLUE *as one who executes robbers waving* STARES away *the gnats* THE five second violence of BLUE *aside balancing* martyrs their tri-sexed blue STARES *how to surprise* THE cleaver cleave to the BLUE *a community* of symmetrical others balancing STARES *somehow it occurred* THE floating Euclidean halo industrialized BLUE *living a public life* Malev lyrical STARES romantic strains of THE distinguished Hungarian lesbian's ivory BLUE cool lost completed no one complained STARES *the original design* THE *was completed no one* BLUE *complained in a few years it was* STARES *forgotten floating it* THE *was framed like any* BLUE *other work of art* as they and their STARES made the only honest choice THE *not too ignobly kicking* BLUE Malev kijárat (exit) *the ladder away* STARES fears of one-way translation THE *now I*

shall tell* BLUE *you* night is grand and crazy STARES out over of THE long short of it BLUE you and/or every blue blade STARES *why it is* THE *beautiful* D'anime nude vidi BLUE in the unheated museum molte gregge STARES welcoming the cleavers THE small smile *design: extraordinary* BLUE *color*: *cobalt blue* (of) *secret platforms* STARES the cold apartment THE *heels twist it into* BLUE *shape* (*it has a*

fantastic area) STARES *made for a* THE *tread that will ascend*
BLUE   orgasme ornithologie semi-solide toi tu tir STARES
Giotto's blue itch THE *being humble i.e. productive* BLUE as
the plants make the sun STARES *its purpose is* THE embouche
fou zigue magnétique BLUE *to take you upward* obsolescent
oracles' STARES reply to coyotes finding THE extreme limit
of   perception BLUE *on an elevator of human fingerprints*
STARES the worse attaches THE better sayings of Spartans
BLUE blue *of the most delicate fixity* STARES *being practical*
for THE animals make the sun BLUE *and*

(us) *knowing its denominator* its STARES la divina vendetta
THE *to push one foot* BLUE philosophers ought to converse
ahead of STARES *the other* inconnu THE stratagems long
aqueducts of BLUE *being a composite sneers at marble*
STARES at the musicologist's THE *all* (of) *orthodox move-*
ments BLUE *discovered in the creak* of now blissed STARES
most sche be THE fa skelts licorice strands BLUE struck *the*
humility of sound that STARES staunch line of THE *spatially*
selective oyster saying BLUE female embryos preparing to
nudge *using* STARES *this counterfeit of* THE

31

height to substantiate a BLUE *method of progress reading stairs as* STARES *an interpolation* of THE as a writer of BLUE essays into *the problem of gradualness* STARES *with a heavy* THE *and pure logic* too BLUE such a blue takes hold of STARES the viewer at THE *the master builder acknowledges* BLUE that blue precisely *this* side of STARES of or beyond THE frightened one then began BLUE *as do the artists in their* STARES *dormer rooms* (of) THE *eternal banishment* hath strekyn BLUE ypon the skye and ledde to STARES *who are usually* THE object's fixed form entailing

BLUE *grateful to anyone who prevents them* STARES short wave-lengths prevail THE before catching the eye BLUE *from taking a false step and* STARES before sunrise serrated
THE first color
to
appear
BLUE *having*
reached the summit
si sentono STARES then
begin again THE *would like to stay*
BLUE not identifying the ob abject sche
STARES into space of THE *even if the stairs*
BLUE sunrise Malev there dotted lines *are withdrawn*

Scientific inquiry, seen in a very broad perspective may
see Foot 1957, also Westermarck 1906, Ch. XIII
To man (sic) the world is twofold, in accordance with
that witness is now or in the future
It wasn't until the waitress brought her Benedictine and she
Villandry, "Les Douves" par Azay le Rideau
mine. Yours, CYNTHIA.
Not a building, this earth, not a cage,
The artist: disciple, abundant, multiple, restless
a forgery: Opus Ioannes Bellini
We named you I thought the earth
is possible I could not tell
to make live and conscious history in common
and wake you find yourself among
and wake up deep in the fruit
Did you get the money we sent?
I smell fire
AT FULL VOLUME. STAGE DARK.]
1. Russia, 1927
God, say your prayers.
You were begotten in a vague war
sidelong into your brain.
In Letter Three & Four (as earlier) the narrator is
North Dakota Portugal Moorhead, Minnesota
The lights go down, the curtain opens: the first thing we
gun, Veronica wrote, the end.
'Wittgenstein'
Tomorrow she would be in America.
Over forty years ago
a tense, cunningly moving tale by the Hunga-
Then he moved on and I went close behind.
Interviewers: What drew a woman from Ohio
to study in Tübingen? American Readers
with this issue former subscribers to Marxist Perspectives
The shadow of the coup continues to hover over Spain

In the ordinary way of summer
girls were still singing
like a saguaro cactus from which any desert wayfarer can draw
as is Mr. Fox, but in literature
Twenty five years have gone by
Ya se dijeron las cosas mas oscuras
The most obscure things have already been said

STEINZAS IN MEDIATION

alighting from the once in a while destroyed it as a momento

Gertrude Stein
"A Vocabulary of Thinking,"
How to Write

There are are there instances of this in every era
A new dispersal of the subject
Or that there shall be a complete fragment
Or that the fragment shall be
As if the is reflects is the
While is the place they were
Between sometimes or what would begin in there here

I.

I And But That In
That But Whatever It And
They But That In Not
In All But Or Not
Made Made Lengthened But But
All Kindly

.

No the river hollow with I call them love
Of up began from who who goes yellow
I must hedge whisper wet going over
Straighten nothing to say un un in
Glassed fill empty burn white

II.

It Or They Or Not
For They Because Coming For
Coming For Or Not But
As Just All All For
More Always Or Just It
As Liking It Once Nearly
In Who They Just Coming
Always Liking Which Mine Or
Often As Think And

.

Of creating a usable past
In here's no where redistributive humor
How to not inscribe yourself in the system you're opposing
Opposing opposable thumbs up to a point of no turn
Not the turn to oppose to it at all

III.
It Yes As To Or
In Please What Not That
Not Coming He He Which
And That As Not Just
It Of She Not And
Or Not She When In
All Or Four And

.

Shades of images of and have read
Instead s/he varied the speeds
Synchronizing mind body as if that were not a problem of no problem
Were willing to leave blanks for to of what not known
No less with than 5 question marks 4 ifs no thens
I gave up Shelley after several years of living in Manhattan.

IV.
Just Or For Which They
It Or Not Nearly For
In All All For They
That In Why For In
That Should All For It
They It It While Should
For For Not No If
Like It But A And
She Did We After They
After Just Once

.

Logic except for instance holding resembling
Wake hold thing thought final hold dissolves holds hold
When word and lives the deep (70 kinds)
As if/no end/so botanist's eye exists
Time sad power error of off or at truant
The view like Chinese poets some goat
West coast realtor sky green chairs rail against
Altitude whats blur from more

V.
Why He All A Tell
Be Be It They In
Let They Better Not In
Not I Land Yes It
Might Did We Because He
Once How All But They
Once He

.

Not to make a famous statement of about clarity
Not to find the famous footprint
Every third thought shall be my grace
Writing synchronizing mind and bodys minds
One wants only clarity yet one wants truth (sic)

VI.
I If If He Namely
Often Left Come They For
Ours Made By In Made
Let But It Because They
Articles Hope Theirs Ever All
For It Just They They
They And With Getting For
It We Who With If
I Of As Not They
They That As Might Just

It This All Aimless She
That Well Or All They
I Gathered All Come See
See Shall

.

In description lies betrayal lies
In descriptions bounded in of or for
What we take as disolution and ruin para phrase
In this out or fall of for next generations to take
For the or a natural order of things
They will not seek their bearings or where we find ours

VII.
Make It For Can For
They Or They Not They
Every She Now There It
Over Famous It By Or
By No They And Or
Which Not Or Or Or
It Might Should Or

.

Better to be amused by your former self
The voila, the hey, the look! alight in the marsh
And here the green I am
Rosy papa flambeau the savage languages
Let's make use of intellectual hindsight
Now in the park the cinematography crew the ruins

VIII.
I Came As Only It
Now Between As There Here
Often It Indicated Just They
Come They They That They

Nobody They I Well Hours
We Imagine He She Or
Or Or It Oh Argued
Which For Will Or Can
Out They More Or They

.

Here are the things I want to remember
Marry doubt fear ought and autocratic
Call this violence a mess polite in language
A thing all shawled well prepared
Once to balance all
The professor sleeps in Bucharest with a gun under her pillow
Out from the whole wide world I chose thee
Necessity combined a treasure
The improving shape of the cloud the cloud disappearing

IX.
With Brush She Or To
They Which That That It
Every

.

"The idea I meant to have"
The problem never was
Only made to brush to call it never playing
People in tanks can't hear each other
Or can't remember a name
Settled and praying better than they will
Once once and for all

X.
Might Even Nor They They
I They Made Might Or
Made It It I Not

But That It That Might
By I Just And If
Just All Not But I
Which But Or In I
Which Or Always Which As
Not For Which Than It
Not I Threads Very I
Neither Might Left Just It
And And And Very Or
Even They I And No
In But Any They Will
Any After Of Once They
As Will In

.

I have thought that the bird makes the same noise differently
Whether we're aware of it or not
Remember dislike reason choose rather happened
Nearly placed they will change in place
Unkind when asked to like it unable to agree
It was for many reasons pale sky green leaves belong to trees
Green leaves just inclined to feel with hope a question
One useless gothic nostril to sniff another full moon
In looking up I have managed to see four things.

XI.
But But Or As In
Of Can Or By Just
Linking Be But Or Finally
In Why They He That
More After Or Or It
An In They Or But
Or They Any Or They
Made Should Without Just By
It Coming Known Think That
I

·

Afternoon eyes diagramming luck
May wish very carelessly pain drifts into hindsight
I have seen what they knew
The feeling of the power of what became mistaken
Or another assumption of we
Many chance encounters with the pain of luck
Or the bird whose call sounds like a telephone ringing
That they call meadows more

XII.
She Not Or Made But
In It All Not One
Or They That Could Just
In It

·

Suppose an invented truth to be slowly dipped in water
They silence in convincing
Moving through the molecules through a beaded curtain
Not alone or only
It is now here that I have forgotten three
Watching it not be left to happen
She said life without theory is Nirvana

XIII.
She By Or Which Or
Just Or Can Made

·

Heat is the motion of a body's parts
Woosh! A new kind of natural law
From romantic clouds to energetic steam
They wish as a button because it is so

XIV.

She They In Come Not
In Should It In Not
That That But Just And
But Or Nobody While Not
To Only This Most It
Just Just It Or It
Than It

.

To compose a life by composing words in a poem
No direct want prevents me
The rain was caught by the hills that were there in the poem
Energy transferred from one thought to another
The she walked out of the they
Right into the foreground to take a bow
To draw an analogy at this point would be obscene
Song is what happens when the mind wanders into time

XV.

Should In But For And
To Which If From In
In In They They And
Whenever Than They Be They
Now And She And All
Once And And That Or
Not By But Not Nor
Should It But They For
Always Is They Not But
Only If As Yes Not
I Or In It For
It And For Or This
They What Not For It
Or That And Probably Alright
And Beginning And When The
And And And And They
Up And I

In why they must see it be there not only necessarily
Finding that crows can count to ten
Come once again come think well of meaning
Once again see there what is there looking reflecting
Must there be another movement now
In which she becomes a he each mourning the other
Suddenly everything seeming elegiac
S/he and all chronically caught in I mean
All speaking all told with capital valor
Yes the alterity of things is an ethical matter
And they can be said to see that at which they look

WITT & STEIN

Witt: In logic nothing is accidental.

Stein: A sentence is a part of the way when they wish to be secure.

Witt: All propositions are of equal value.

Stein: A sentence is an interval during which if there is a difficulty they will do away with it.

Witt: If there is any value that does have value, it must lie outside the whole sphere of what happens and is the case. For all that happens and is the case is accidental.

Stein: A sentence is their politeness in asking for a cessation. And when it happens they look up.

To compose thoughts using logics and propositions and sentences is accidental like all that happens and is the case for it is the case that all that happens is accidental and all that is accidental is contingent but never arbitrary and it happens and is the case that values are composed in sentences and propositions that are accidental and are (therefore) (themselves) accidental and contingent and never arbitrary.

A sentence is a proposition during which if there is a difficulty there will be value since value is contingent on noticing and noticing occurs only when there is a difficulty. Much that happens and is the case and is accidental happens and is the case and is accidental in the intervals before after during between and among those propositions called sentences and those sentences called propositions.

Any accident that does have value must lie inside the sphere of what happens and is the case for all that happens and is the case is accidental and has accidental value. All that lies outside the sphere of what happens and is the case lies inside the sphere of the sentence that proposes what happens and does not happen, what is and is not the case and is (therefore) (equally) accidental.

All propositions are of equal value is a proposition that may or may not be valued equally with the proposition that all propositions are not of equal value. Whether or not it or they are valued happens and is the case and is (therefore) accidental. These propositions are of value only because they are the case and are accidental and lie inside the whole sphere of what happens and is the case and is accidental.

To compose these thoughts using propositions is accidental like all things that happen and are the case. For the composition of anything that becomes the case happens and is accidental. This accident of what happens and is the case has equal value with what does not happen and is not the case. For all that happens and is the case is accidental. And all that does not happen and is not the case is accidental.

A sentence is an accident during which if there is any value there will be a difficulty. This proposition is a sentence that is an interval during which if there is a difficulty they may or may not do away with it.

An interval is a value in noticing what happens. That it is noticed is the case and is accidental and is its value. (Therefore) value is an accident of noticing and is the case and exists inside the sphere of all that happens and is the case with all that lies outside the sphere of what happens and is the case. An accident in which there is a proposition like all things that happen is always coincidental with an accident in which there is no proposition.

An accident that is called a they is a coincidence of noticing.

What may happen and therefore may be the case is an accident that has not yet happened and is not and may never be the case and is therefore a difficulty no one can do away with.

If all propositions are of equal value, a sentence which is an interval during which there can be a difficulty must lie outside the whole sphere of what has happened and is the case and must do away with equal value.

If there is a difficulty in composing thoughts using sentences that are accidental like all things that happen and are the case they may or may not notice and may or may not do away with it.

If there is any value that does have value it must be noticed in the interval between what has happened and is the case and what has not happened and may never be the case. For all that has value and is the case is accidental and will (therefore) be accidental and when it happens they may look up.

i.e., a sentence is a *lapdog palm* during which they will *no próblem* if and only if *unannounced intentions creepy arithmetic* and *denotation withered on the vine* during which *no próblem* during which which *a mount* is a proposition during which if there is a difficulty there will be *no próblem rebus trigger correspondent strife* during which if and only if *melancholy Leafy Mélisande ecclésia mega ton storm no próblem* during which difficulty they *tepid ten off demon geese* is an interval a difficulty in which if and only if *no próblem motor dapple clip lapdog* reaching *no próblem* across *no próblem unannounced intentions rebus trigger* triggers *no próblem* a difficulty difficulty if and only if *Leafy Mélisande* and/or *no próblem melancholy geese* during which *exit máp-bell* if and only if difficulties will *no próblem Whitman táp-dance* during which *no próblem* no difficulty *no próblem California laptop* sentence *demon* preposition of *no próblem melancholy whistle-pork* sentence & proposition reach *no próblem* across to *no próblem Depth misfortune no próblem* if and only if happenstance can dictate *active tympani lip*

ARCHIMEDES' NEW LIGHT
Geometries of Excitable Species

Mortals are immortals and immortals
mortals; the one living the other's death
and dying the other's life.

Heraclitus

bodies cleave space of   all the triangles in the prism :

one glimpse of cornered sky in   all the triangles in the sphere :

fleeing over cardboard mountain with   all the segments in the parabola :

grey morning blank aluminum   all the parabolas in the sphere :

their own cold love song breached   all the circles of the sphere :

abrupt start of rain   all the vertices of the prism :

clacking sticks
night barks
window blank

Reason is a daemon in its own right.

another song whose bird I do not know
.the.center.of.gravity.of.the.two.circles.combined.
around them in us we were very they
what comes to mind in this five second cove
.whose.diameters.are.and.when.their.position.is.
.changed.hence.will.in.its.present.position.be.
lacking usage equal to the noun she chose
.in.equilibrium.at.the.point.when.all.the.angles.
all different before he heft laughed defiled gravity lost again
.in.the.triangles.in.the.prism.all.the.triangles.in.the.cylinder.
interior angles exposed collapsed into each each
.section.and.the.prism.consists.of.the.triangles.in.
the terrible demonstration of fluid dynamics beginning again
.the.prism.hence.prism.hence.also.the.prism.and.the.
areas of distortion the burning vector fields

more mathematics of the
unexpected:
the total curvature of all
spheres
is exactly the same regardless
of radius

Lacking experience equal to the adjective she chose
scratch abstract sky shape
hoping for more

> .whole.prism.containing.four.times.the.size.of.the.
> .other.prism.then.this.plane.will.cut.off.a.prism.from.

struggle to flee her altered nativity
repeat story of stilt accident
no the drama has not abated

> .the.whole.prism.to.circumscribe.another.composed.
> .of.prisms.so.that.the.circumscribed.figure.exceeds.

exhausted boy soldier reads book numb
rag head taken by stiff light
fig one triumph of the we're

> .the.inscribed.less.more.than.any.given.magnitude.
> .but.it.has.been.shown.that.the.prism.cut.off.by.the.

empty listen ridge cold whistle
unison whipped wide awake
box of spook salt

> .inclined.prism.the.plane.the.body.inscribed.now.in.
> .the.cylinder-section.now.the.prism.cut.off.by.the.

not a coast but a horizon not a coast
blank seas soak grain senses demented
sense of thigh once now not yet juked

> may deter may
> bruise
> bequeath before
> death
> green countdown
> bluebook

she said now that she thought about it
she thought it must have had something
to do with that feeling of self possession in
the moment after the apostrophe took hold

One's   .inclined.plane.the.body.inscribed.in.the.cylinder.

a stock image
a rhetorical device
a dubious gesture
an obsolete hope

One's   .section.the.parallelograms.which.are.inscribed.in.

quadrant spoke motion
a prod to come to life
meddlesome meaning meaning tangent

One's   .the.segment.bounded.by.the.parabola.but.this.is.

sordid alignment of slippery parts
please hold that place stretch the we
jelly throat made good hold that note

One's   .impossible.and.all.prisms.in.the.prism.cut.off.by.the.

---

no such five illusions
no vowel exit mutters fruit
my no flute war
torque valley breath
gun cold air cont'd
night barks windows blank
grey morning's blank aluminum
its own long cold burst that kills
a look cornered sky

One's   .inclined.plane.all.prisms.in.the.figure.described.

geometry of the tragic spectrum
eye caught in grid
this thought empties itself in false déjà vu
the echo seen but not heard
the absence of x had been distracting all along

.around.the.cylinder.section.all.parallelograms.in.the.
.parallelograms.all.parallelograms.in.the.figure.
.which.is.described.around.the.segment.bounded.
.by.the.parabola.and.the.straight.line.the.prism.cut.
.off.by.the.inclined.plane.the.figure.described.around.
.the.cylinder.section.the.parallelogram.the.figure.
.bounded.by.the.parabola.and.the.straight.line.
.the.prism.the.prism.cut.off.by.the.inclined.plane.

LOST BRIEF CASE CONJECTURE

do not give up on me us you them
lucky lucky number number number
the sky is always the hardest
blue in the beginning
wasabi chance chance wasabi wasabi sunset
it's all true all lucky lucky
lucky lucky lucky numbers are blue
drawing on the past on blue blue
instance
the sky is always the hardest
left with all these these
those numerical objects
not there at the time
no yes important yes manuscript lost
the brief case suit case back pack valise is left
in the elevator taxi Alps Pyrenees garage hotel room locker bar
on the bench train bus ferry trolley counter street
at the station news stand terminal border ATM
blue blue wasabi number can you be can you be factored into
primes
does an opinion occupy space
can the Imperial flora look beautiful ever again
(nothing left on the right clock)
does the rise into ruin be or be come the sky

COIMBRA POEM OF POETRY AND VIOLENCE

GRIEF'S RUBIES

Joan Retallack & Forrest Gander

May 24, 2007–June 29, 2008

rendezvous of the pronouns
days of earaches dies irae in re in re
paradox of the Loire (dark elbows)
la cantatriste brioche and / or omelet hurricanes
the little verb is present
the better to catch les mouches
tears before the robe (blear) come
the raunchy men the good and violent men
the beautiful and fearful children the women the
pretty drawings of the house, the tree, the
chicken the
gorgeous women on the escalator
feeling the fusion again and again
watch the soufflé (death and pleasure)
the future of silence (base canard misnomer)

Both piss-out and motive to continue. To advance the pearl, its globe, that lapidary fixation cemented to strangeness. And grief's rubies. Egged on and on. A durance opened wide and collared to a rose, at the ear. Divined or smug, êtes vous écoutant? Later, museum quality sex. But you are not done yet.

United alphabet conferred by silent riverine dark. Mortality: a pastoral.
Slowly, small river of protest. Love refrains. Flood-buckled.

one thing I must explain to you (aria)
now for the rest (recitative)
Creek King—I am the big I am big I the big
set of three, rustling match
pulmonary minuet
custard thunder clap
(lost all sense of time)

Candled meadows don't know us. Torrential piano. Always a beyond to the finality of the act.

> nachos tempos para normal fiesta (the eggs) gracias
> daughter of mellow Brahmins and Mercatos
> the rest stop cara via man drowned the rabbits
> the whole thing forcèd umbrella morte seculares
> in the chantine, in Berlin, in a church in a church

lipo lipida lipidus historica
tout-o-bus the roxy hear-o-horn
omnisota search engine toxipoeta
enervita aporia toxicola
meet me in Kenya (it's my surname)
ride the little verb to market
but don't squash it
and don't eat it
and don't hurt it
it has feelings to it
it to it it takes you here
say thanks to it and good night to it
someday I'll read to you the rest of it

...with a leak in it, or a leak through it, equally paralyzing, illing me, what an early savageness, heaped on it, high on it, anaesthetizing, verying me.

Flowing through the ossature of moon-dice, temporal money. A remittance antique and rococo. Consuming the divine Maria, pressed to dust, so more spheroidal. Lamentable mustache over guava—regarded as a malicious mirage. Tired of miracles not spiders, these she waits for. In a dark like a museum or bush, surprised.

dish dis-pen named à bientôt
when is the day quantas over
omni and over and terra silenta
Fiji who gotten she (pregnant) Maria sparrow
into the book in Vienna in spiritus
undo undo Zumundo undo this sanctus
brilliant Maria-Jacques oudit outfit
mañana mundo the fused ray of off
saints dressage todo mundo sexcuse
this is the room where the private act will take
place
(Socrates is our president)

ow ter damn
oh too
oooose ah
fingers flying
meatonahook
in der haus elk came in
hunderwasserkunst de bella dia
(please, where is the Debussy?)
mandelbrotten in damnmark
just trying to understand
O mea mea stacked liederhausen liederlich
a lump a lump ear infected six bells sounding
the reader's dramatic inflection
now here
Rambo's Rimbaud
if we live   only the name   the stain of it

Get thee out of that hole, spoke. Get thee out of the earth, spoke by black cedar. Optic vole. Leaning near dangling, very very long, and then shoveled the dirt in. Myopic little man endowed with what did I say? Well, I. The mound left glowing like a mitt, bell six bonging. Who, blind as the meristem, bowed to avoid it. Blown under rocks, a noun. Unlunged by day. Driven until he hooted at its demand.

Accepting the flattery of the Mediterranean, even its nasty tempos, on the john, spectacular and otherwise occupied by *Daktari* or arrested. What a cost, cooperating. I was scared, typical quote. Jail tricks and theatrum, then something more. Nautical domestics, a saturate emporium—*The light!* she whispers. Like a China spring.

> coffee rain bells
> not possible to pass through this thought again
> dedicated to speranza in Italian
> how to translitterate less is more into morels
> the explosion ejected the hand
> they consulted the dictionary of world religions

glut of syllables
zip up your sides
best delights of sputum
(fixed smile)
buckeye mordre ordre
buggoff Russian farina
fuckeye olive order   kaboom
(dog ciao)
crusted dove horror show
(cossacks knee Luigi)
Old Exclamatory Proverb: All the baskets and only one egg!
inconsonanti inconsolable
the masculine member and its sculpture in the museum in Rome
all contained in
3 small poems w/ dots and dashes over all the vowels

Rat poison goiter below the geezer's jawline, smallpox and buggered. Is that gummy caramel radish—pardon me, he said, smearing the probe on my crown, smearing my sleeve. Eat more milk? he stole a look at me. An acid leak across my pulse. Risky caprice it was. I cried in a nasal tune, Oh vicious gladiola, the solution's not polite.

A yogurt ditty while we postpone the last act of tragedy? Affected as a wax nose, mistress of novices not allowed to point out devastations disguised as progress, barking mad, while others jaded with exertion have died barking.

a real laer is not a reel leer
neither a woman stepping off a cross I should say
Joan The Meatless of Norridge
(Blake occurs now)
walking down the hill in Moscow to the river chance
(fly flies by)
he looked at me one day in Umbria
(folly)

mort-23 times
mother ferocious raucon sexus copse to corpse
Alberto the terrorist and malingering squash
players
misogynistas sobs and pools of sobs
how sad how sad-52 times
what vipers what vipers-64 times

...enduring grasses of anguish, American anguish mashed to the windshield with fruit called the future. Such an anguine shine. Fastened to an ambush in September, but prudent as Zurich. A beach I don't care to share with your vacation, captain of whiskey and a cargo of prunes. Charged with never blowing a tuba I was back to the grasses who know me. While in a blaze of shells, a combine.

Internal bonanza, the small suave raconteur at the disco devoted as a moth to chamois: come, if your education hoots not, you'll pee on the dessert, so to say. My companion, Tonto, Sir, Amen. Who traverses the pissage with valor or ennui, holding his lapels. Enthusiasm seconds me. In the company of one orange. Whose orange visage vaccinated the bizarre fondue in the CEO's lap. No dumb accident if you regard the avenue.

this (poem) (is) about me
dish (of) (the) nebulae

elegy for Robert Creeley
is it a far off bird or a floater
the desert border of the palimpsestina
here the plumpest border of the sestina
far off bird I too am a floater
for Bob the elegy is Creeley

A photograph taken in a zinnia, voltage through the patella dips goes the saying, limping over so-and-so's mother. – 'ts the matter?

Whose face—a falling beat—like alfalfa, sad, or roche moutonnée. And whose escape from the shoe by a fascicle in the freezage, or crèche, was magnific. That radish of a dauphin in pause between bites, blinking, white as a star. He enters, improvised like autumn's zeal. Who had seen the shade-drawn sadness firing serum light, an event sultry as a house. To which I object to less. Still objecting to the wattage, the day lapping.

            salt soap improvèd fragrant ouvroir
            financial corpu para mirroir
            with schoole folke he standishe siche
            shamata salle salle or crèche
            salle or crèche or sea level quiche
            long heart break the sequel
            afternoon of the song
            constroy agon dia comme un pop
            frosh viva representing (life)
            awash palaver j'aime desperately Tennessee Williams
            and Pushkin too another doughnut smasher
            Hippolyte spector of Spanish
            Ashbery sing no such thing
            you my mucho loudo sensate figura Schpeck the Cat
            condense lotso ich-sweetass in search of dias
            dio tiempo rest aria non say plus much
            downwind King Charles
            über seviche

How about that syllabus! Inside the jaw of a cow. Who pried the coarse mouth? Usually you find larger meters. In the last eclipse, palpitating, I gather he suffered from alto-morose. Day-baggage. Hootchie-coochie. A fetish guy came by, and a madrigal pear.

>remove a pessoa
>a qui karaoke diablo
>nail sore Gail Faust
>nuevo mooda impressive silence
>merde Johnny Cavalcante from the old
>corpu
>anchante forma quatro eclipse
>threw sugar at my shadow
>cabbage for the voyage voyage a map a
>veranda
>is it possible to make sense of the music
>of love
>the shame of the mind (boy pogrom)
>je me plage in spiritu dunko

spellate
auto scheggiate
rap for gliders
todo el día
avec picolo me grande
avec skin-a-norte
vista tutto (ah) all amazing
fructo Pennsylvania
mio zio is a kind of wine
and now for the intrusion in Italiano
violent torte ludica
hum 3 bars, then cough
first I mistake the railing for the horizon
then the assumption of the version
vorrei brava capitano di mondo

Mark them marchers and soap the beast, alarmed or lashed with invective, whose pain of yoke-skinned docity—don't fuck with Pennsylvania! You won't stand the mode, the terrible event echo, no, go repent to a pure mutism, shed the crepuscular jet set accustomed to a familiar burro called Lorca in a cast—what a scandal, and with applause.

Indentured leader pretending like unto a dormant fish, what more, broom in sand, an aluminum bark oozing finitude, another decrepit itinerary of violent natality.

fatigued corpus (in Korea?)
to the hope depth of the sky
in terror of lattes
in fruition more cantos tristes
cosa morta care flicked off
crickets tear at pompous deli

the world of Alice is all that is encased
the angled fault of water hounds
with the wisdom of Goethe
save the foyer
gedanken wizzened shaft
mere Alice riced and diced
pain   night tag   eine b)

Underland chimes christen flies in the kingdom of ants. I'm given straight Balthus. Show me. Sell the hide. Sell the house without a sheet. Erred for your dad's goof. A tour of the shaft elemental. Sell the water. Sell the roof. Never the eucalyptus. Docent eyes infested with light, the dark city victim, darkly stricken, wanders through Eva's flat.

So mill me. Tariff me. Small-tariff me, my raccoon. Phosphor and salty porn belie us. Whatever the answer-washer, it's iridium or sybariticum, you decide. I only half embrace what follows in the utterance of your eye.

                                    frankly frank
                                    I don't like to read in English
                                    you have your Cézanne

questa vamoosa William Blaka
blink to see the world in a grain of sand
black nas pareles parodia graffitas
Tasi con violencia Blake's dos equi
mestastis bienale grazia Caspar todos
block expensimentos giaconda marijauna
Africanes seculo bleak secular cadenzas
les negres tempora soba the font is instrumental
for the music the hope the justice
tremendous solidarity
children of wolves don't step on a wolf
howl now
or say your prayers

Exude the future, is set. It's clear, no bets. And if you can, with saliva in
your ear—

Or a somber pest, half-starved, enormous. A poultice of music relents into visibility. It stinks up my event, stupid with hope. You don't battle a nest with memories. Spartan shadows falling on the east terrace, Corinthian ruins. In a bath of phosphorescence, three candidates. Cult auroras foment the gravid and cancerous nose, nose of light I'll bet you. And scumbling the ceviche.

free god Aida
because becomes you with gusto
Fernande y Fernando rowing in or out
to sea
it is not that it does not exist

America Latina assassinata
lumaresque identificazione in oz
org ozone sonata tico und une bête
ascend the penis while all is flowing downward
(names of all the great authors here)

Incorrect, straight cash. Just pretend. A parasite for you. Vertical each ladder tap. Insolent or like a machine squint. Then begotten for the camera, an onslaught of self, onslaught of latest seller, of pawn, oboe meeting sea, when at the brink of injurious freshness, too intense—oh gone! Prescient vicissitude on a walker and I know no climbing back. I missed the torrent, the sliding tide, presaged, crystalline, I floated by on the bottom of supplication. Stamen of the world mashed flat.

Fabulous enough. Chin-ups. Goose flesh institute. What kind of hole? Walk on now, she said. Star trekker. A tiny male entered a mole hole. Ha ha. Quiet, will you! His dusty potion lifted into a lingo. I apologize, welcome in, drop it there. Ashes. Can you go, tongue in snafu. Plus the honeybee— who is that worth for? Wipe up, whiney! Tongue straight out, soldier.

        tien tien lego finito
        tangerine mispronounced is tincture juncture
        Ginsberg island inside thin chin
        numzero   hugo sensed it
        tangy shoe shoe fly oh tedious cook
        elm tincture à la low tea
        you tease me you shimmy true
        you snafu ing ing
        sanguine shirt of Il Yenko Ginko
        guillotine trainometer set up
        Tieniamin waterland kills dasein fast
        wing or fairy   yin or wing
        afix the kosher machine

poetry niche beast clamor
auto car me impressa
desperado inflamado
ludicrous moon in the poem
ludicrous tree, bird, death, life in the poem
equal art daring sofa
gnosh violet with pleasure
other name or other name scenario
another student of a moment of silence
subterranean mart peche impasse
terra familia all foreign and sincere
seep tarriff eschkimow explodes without warning
déjà corpse meringue villa
substituto strange planet (not ours) (shameless)
this is about death vacuole green ink infanta the licorice canto the fall into

Not the petrol gang! (Not the petrol gang). No violent rehash. Whose nose
was largest? The plural of it is. When we arrive at balsamic silence. When
the distance of others, as on the phone. When the mouth terror. When the
workshop shed is hung with thin meat. When we go brown with waiting. It
pertains to slash and fabrication. Standing in despair. Farm fresh creams.

WESTERN CIV CONT'D

And then Tortoise said to Hare, *Slow down
Bo Peep, we're all in this together, right?*

Hare replied, *I think you've mistaken me
for someone else, my good woman. Among
other things, you've got the wrong story,
the wrong gender, and the wrong species.
I gotta go.*

What other things? cried Tortoise as the
horizon disappeared in a cloud of dust.

1.

First find the pulse / just fish'n in a nuclear age / BTW what DID Beowulf,
Hamlet, & Little Red Riding Hood have in common / 4251 BC/E History
begins / repeats itself / tragedy farce tragedy farce farce farce tragédie-farci
here we go again / pull up those argyle socks for happy days despite loss of
elevated language, dial time, etc / BE the change, etc / clockwise is knowing
your place in time / 3500 BC/E harps & flutes played in Egypt / and then
she says, Like Hell! (Let me introduce myself) / yes, of course, she & he,
this and that and always more and less they come (all of them) & go w/ th
spd of snd & lt & we in them move with them toward history / this is what
I want to have happened / thinking of them, our children approach with the
grace of sound and light / no need to rehearse next installment / hold on
don't let go / get it down quick / 3000 BC/E lyres & double clarinets
played in Egypt / graffiti bombardiers nothing new / you can't spend the
rest of your life staring at the horizon her mother said / stare at the horizon
& the horizon becomes you – the horror, etc / c'mon get up / let's go /

2.

Instructions as follows: more & more signs & codes (they love to decipher)
as trains roll through the Bronx MR SEEN illuminates 24 hr DAY-GLO-
NITE / today it hit all 5 boroughs / I just wanted people to know I exist he
said when interviewed on TV / we're all in this together, right, just hang'n
out, try'n to survive / only the day before 2500 BC/E Pepi wrote instruc-
tions to his son: go to school, act w/ dignity, hold that impulse / Hap + Pen
from anglo 'quirk of luck' + saxon 'slip of tongue' / long of arm, short of
tongue, Cornish man lost his land / 2700 BC/E court musician Ling-lun
plays first bamboo flute in China / Sumerians drinking mineral water for
their health / run they cried run faster than your shadow or you'll never get
away / 365 day calendar introduced 2772 BC/E / polished metal mirrors
inspire unprecedented acts of vanity / dogs already pets in Egypt / throughout
the literature lamentations & skepticism about the meaning of life / Upshift
& Overcome Honey Bun / Ancient Egyptian Story: they trembled &
quaked in their BC/E-ness fearing the goddess would destroy mankind / but
she got drunk and it was good in her heart and she found a still pond and
her face (appeared) beautiful therein and took no further notice of mankind
/ quick pull down the shades pull on your speedo suit make big splash or
quick getaway /

3.

On the other side of history pictures of skiers carved on rocks in Norway c.
2300 BC/E / Bisquick Bug Bomb interurban line's beady-eyed vanishing
points popping up everywhere / no more compound vision no more poly-
phonic rhythms / words come vulgar and gregarious as headless chickens
in the backyards of Babylon / c. 2000 BC/E dough rises dough sets except
when you're on the run / Eat Drink This is my Body as they say in the
new-fangled liturgy / Why *my* generation? they asked / fast-growing trees
seemed desirable / more Shake & Bake Desperate Art / more land grabs
and ancient grudges and internecine wars / She would (according to Jane
Kramer) watch for the train and think about her weekly bet, and about
her honeymoon and the *pension* at Lourdes where she discovered how
disappointing love was compared to mass in the grotto, or the sight of a ton
of corn filling the family's orange metal crib after a good harvest / mass
migrations of displaced peoples, loss of loved ones and homelands and
innocent consolations / despite loss of luggage now and then I love to fly,
he said / I like the way I and it rise all together above everything / when I
was a child I saw the movie of *Hamlet* / I couldn't believe it when Hamlet
died / he didn't seem like the type /

4.

Suddenly it's 1480 BC/E again and Queen Hatshepsut rules for her son
Thutmose III until his coming of age / just looking / trying to give reasons
for the fate that is in us plus or minus one or two retrospective bright ideas
/ don't worry you can't miss it it's as big as a barn / lips purse in the cliché
on the face / here's what the future holds: great explosion of meaning,
dialectical tension, structural integrities no longer debased / the most exquisite
thought of the word *plumb* moistened her lips and eyes / she would watch
the child walk run slip away from her even as she drew the child near in
her sight / it was morning August 6, 1945 / the story of Sinuhe the Lucky
Man had been recounted and written down and lived by in Egypt since
1550 BC/E / In the story as Sinuhe approached his death he came upon a
large house / In the house was a cool room and images of the horizon all
around / now no next generation / No, that can't be true! / the phone is
ringing in the next frame & /

5.

For a long time I used to believe that Twinkies had a shelf life longer than the lifespan of the Common Loon / Sometimes when I had put aside thoughts of trumpets in Denmark 1500 BC/E my eyes would close to dreams of the Spectacled Eider on the other side of the lens / Marconi and his South Wellfleet wireless brought beads of sweat to many a forehead a smile to many a careworn face / c. 1903 static picked up one big bang after another / *In taking advantage of the wonderful triumph of scientific research and ingenuity which has been achieved in perfecting a system of wireless telegraphy, I extend on behalf* / black cats from the pelt farm just walked off the island when the channel froze / Egyptians rt abt cats — no dummies / skilled telegraphers sent out messages at 17 words per minute / Voice of America began broadcasting overseas / but the sea cliff of South Wellfleet was eroding at a rate of 3 ft a year / 17 words a minute times 3 ft a year = 1916 eastern-most towers threatened with collapse / 1500 BC/E percussion added to Egyptian orchestras / across the street a bird takes flight with a worm in its mouth at the precise moment the lawn mower starts up and her husband falls dead upon the unmown grass / cause & effect run away with the spoon / elegy eclogue eulogy epitaph encomium in memoriam Narcissus and Echo / wake up it's getting late do you really want to sleep your life away /

6.

2000 BC/E palace at Minos has light & air shafts bathrooms w/ running
water / contraceptives freely used in Egypt / tonight 30% chance of rain
intermittent thunderstorms flood watch extinctions taking place all the time
/ it's hard not to think of myself as the center of the solar system, he says,
being entertained by all the planets & stars / 1500 BC/E Moses leads
Israelites out of Egypt nabs 10 commandments, etc / what's the value of
absolute number here? / is Judeo-Christian morality really a decimal affair
? / much later a privileged few will be trained to locate the point and come
to it / wine corky tonight / Troy destroyed 1193 BC/E / Hindu numerals
first to include zero 8th c. CE / Fibonaci writes *Liber Abaci* 4 centuries
later / what to make of all this odd timing / we've come to the moment of
our birth as to an important meeting in the nick of time hoping only to
sleep like a top / vanilla egg cream eclogue / fireproof Hittite library tablets
in 8 languages / history is toast long before & after Alexandria / guitars
lyres trumpets tambourines egrets herons anhingas, rivers sing as they flow
now as in 300 or 1500 or 5000 BC/E / hurry up, more elegies needed now
than ever before / boom boom pity poor Bikini Islands, Hiroshima,
Nagasaki, Crab Nebula fizz, special effects ergo sum / one might at any
moment in the course of it ask what the hell's going on / enormously witty
epitaph pending for 1500 BC/E alone / wait / off to gas station & liquor
store / be back /

7.

SOON superhighway eulogies in pink convertibles / it was or is already c.
1956 / Sexy Propertius & his gal Cynth in Living Green Exotica / Corn
Flakes, Wheaties, Quaker Oats found to be good for you / first Chinese
dictionary 40,000 characters c. 1450 BC/E / Persians wearing tight leather
clothes / comes moon 1st fat then skinny / seasons skinny fat / as the world
turns I blow my nose uniting commonplace and cosmic / cosmi-comics guy
of no fixed gender in tattersall shirt breaking & entering / "Poetry is break-
ing and entering" s/he tossed over a left shoulder as s/he left older and
wiser no doubt / Where were you all this time, damn you? / species vanishing,
mailings out to that effect / The Plymouth Gentian The Roseate Tern The
Marbled Salamander The Golden Club / I like the sound of the word *piss,*
she said, though I was born in Vienna / on a quiet day you could hear the
sound of an Amish buggy or a cow pissing a mile & a half away / but /
wait / we're talking China 1450 BC/E / we're talking all those characters &
The Dining Philosophers Problem /

....

Breakdance Lecture: I remember him to have said "I" immediately. It was
the first thing he said. This is no doubt oversimplification. One of those
highways that's replaced a neighborhood.

....

8.

The Dining Philosophers Problem: 5 philosophers seated at a round table in a Chinese restaurant have only 5 chopsticks among them. They must establish a pattern of eating and philosophizing that allows 2 philosophers to eat at any given time t with one chopstick remaining unused where all 5 philosophers will have had equal time $t-1$ to eat & philosophize by the time $t-2$ all the food is gone. They are eating Steamed Dumplings, Hunan Chicken, Ginger & Scallion Whole Yellowtail, Szechuan Stringbean with Rice / 1300 BC/E properties of Pythagorean triangle known in China (Hypatia—wife of Pythagoras—credited posthumously) / Also, Cold Sesame noodles, Hot 'n Sour Soup /

....

Breakdance Lecture cont'd: It used to make me sick when my neighbors didn't like me. I'd have nightmares about it. Even when I didn't like them. Since there was so much I didn't know about myself, there was always the possibility they were right. There, "I" have said it. (to be cont'd)

....

9.

Labor strike in Thebes c. 1300 BC/E sale of beer regulated in Egypt / It will have taken the invention of the computer to invent & solve The Dining Philosophers Problem / (Just what was that problem anyway?) / Food was good, right? / WHAMMO POW! Oxo Reaction / very short exposure could cause injury or death / BUT / this was never meant to be a life-saving device / one squeeze dispenses one drop / do not use in case of emergency / Subway Ad: HOW TO: 1) improve your vocabulary 2) write with style 3) enjoy the classics 4) use a library 5) enjoy poetry 6) spell / FLIPSIDE: more musical moments or the Chinatown blues / COMING SOON: money - sex - clothes - food - cars - dreams - women - men - tv - fame - more good & bad habits - more wars - new flavors - record breaking sales / 1000 BC/E rationalism on rise in China / has it all come to this / or that / MR SOON not yet too late / water filled cubes measure time / memories - anecdotes - stories - tales - lies (this fiction I have _____ed against my ruin) wanting, needing / travelogues & slide shows / sneak attacks / five and seven-tone scales in Babylonian music coming up / more & more names of places you've never been /

10.

200 years of chaos c. 1000-800 BC/E / mass migrations of Germanic peoples / Philistines attack Palestine / would distinction between wanting & needing have made a difference in any of this? / 900 BC/E Chinese math book includes proportion, planimetry, arithmetical rule of three, root multiplication, equations with unknown quantities, theory of motion geometry / unisex clothes soon to appear in Assyria / uncounted species spring up and disappear / class antagonisms continue in Greek countryside 800-600 BC/E / in geography class c. 1950 CE they learned Yugoslavia is world's leading manufacturer of safety pins, the music of the folk is neither raucous nor disturbing, the people are warm & friendly, etc / why did we have to learn all that when the country no longer exists / *O Mensch bewein dein Sunde gross* (just call me Billie Blue) / already when very small she had noticed scissors and trousers analogous / COMING SOON improvements to many things not yet inklinged or conceived /

11.

....

Breakdance Lecture cont'd: The trouble is I don't know how to get rid of it
– the *I* – what to do instead. *We* seems pretentious. *She* seems schizo-
phrenic. (the end)

....

As for transportation, those people not driven out of their lands often
wished to go to many places on round-trip tix / valences vectors tendencies
desires on the move / the future tense will never be suppressed / e.g., don't
talk like the Bronx you'll get out of the Bronx / it was long thought that the
sole purpose of the brain was to cool the blood / Aristotle said as much c.
400 BC/E) / now, with war following war, one might think perhaps he had
a point / more recently, she considered it might be better to be notorious
than unknown and therefore thought of killing her husband knowing her
chances of getting the elusive book contract would be much improved from
the proverbial jail cell / there were of course other reasons for wanting to
kill her husband / Hi Gloria! Hi Ed! / Syrian soldier depicted with Egyptian
wife & son c. 1300 BC/E / Homer and their ilk will refer to highly sophisti-
cated battlefield surgery c.800 BC/E / in Greece crafts and trade flourish
as farmers starve /

12.

1000 BC/E Song of Songs begins, hits sour note / it's not that I don't like
fast food, s/he said, I do I do like fast food / Accht! Library books overdue!
/ *Odyssey* shown to justify class dominance by military landowners viz
Enough of your eloquence you drivelling fool, Odysseus shouts, *How dare
you stand up to the king!* / but Song of Songs' erotic content makes for
sticking power / miles-o-smiles & margarine, land-o-lakes internecine /
Pinto Indians building loam covered huts in Sierra Nevada 900 BC/E / seas
full of tunny, anchovy & sardine / Is that right, Mildred, she said, eyes
squinched, raising cigarette in air / things are getting more and more com-
plicated all the time or so it seems / try to focus, listen for nasal release of
stop consonant in *eaten   sudden   mitten* / must learn to be cool-headed
convivial convincing courageous, to mention only the Cs / 1OOO-900
BC/E wigs popular among aristocrats in Assyria and Egypt / Israelis adopt
caftan / poppies growing all over Middle East / SOON Rosenbergs electro-
cuted McCarthy show goes on tv / when it rains we're all equal she said / I
remember her saying that like it was yesterday / when it rains, she coun-
tered, some fear more than others being cold & wet & flooded out of their
homes / you expected consistency? /

13.

You may remember *O Mensch* (sic) *bewein* (no vibrato) cosmi-toss whims of
this or that mini-epoch / cosmetic smiles prophylactc frowns concerted grins
twinkle toes / all this and more fully explained in coming installments /
sudden movement produces flashes or glints of light:

     breathe in . . . . . .gentian breakdance water cube time
     breathe out . . . . already it's never been later

CIRCA ANCIENT TIMES

Chinese invent wheelb
ATTRACTOR) so much
kite water cube time /
Chinatown appear?) /
about what is known a
to strangeness and bac   FIG.13

arrow (MIND AS STRANGE
depends upon this precursor
(when does first déjà vu or
not everything known
t any given time / charm turns
k to charm without warning

14.

Hey! just one more thing before scribe or data entry type makes yet another error / (foolish particle waves to crowd) / i.e., not certain how long we can go on this way so let's just creep up on ourselves / Pythagorean Triangle known in China approx 1000 yrs before birth of Pythagoras / Dear child! / collective memory fails again nothing new / Spinoza sooner or later will (have) conclusively demonstrate(d) emotions nothing but inadequate ideas / topology of the glance: a. stab air with index finger b. enter your point / the truth about history may be a matter of indifference for history / does this throw doubt on need for truth? / allusion, reference, Obs. / s/he shrugged / sighed / yearned as they all forgot for millennia that the earth is round nonetheless living w/ the consequences / forgetting too that Crow polo was played coed / what with the uncanny force of science – if truth is really a strange experimental fiction then experiment may render that fiction real / e.g., Carthage using concrete in search of good life viz in search of pleasure domes and sturdy columns / you can now enter your opening monologue on the competition site / you can now contemplate with serene decorum the stately plump two-handled jars of brandy and lovely mares in Homer /

15.

Ah the sun saturated bliss just before a squall comes up in the Aegean or the Chesepeake Bay / Clytemnestra feels it in her crotch / Agememnon realizes he's a jerk / Antigone goes on Oprah for the umpteenth time / dearest Athena, sun-bleached goddess of justice, we're glad we didn't know you when you were that painted harlot in a garish Parthenon / only a few minutes after takeoff the earth turned blue / everybody laughed and cried / it didn't last / Victor Hugo thought being buried in Père La Chaise would be living for eternity with the finest mahogany furniture / bullet enters exit / explosion heard as from a great distance / and then, the story goes, in the blink of an eye justice did prevail / hard to put a date on these things / Queen Hatshepsut glues on beard and goes to work like any other man /

....

Breakdance Lecture cont'd: *I* spent the first half of *my* life being precocious; now *I*'m spending the second half being a late bloomer. But things could be worse. Marty's uncle invested $10,000. in a circus in Sarasota Florida. A week later the lead elephant died. Nobody knew what to do. The body became a public health hazard as it decomposed in a city park. The circus went bankrupt. "John, you were born to suffer," his third wife said. Marty's uncle never lost his nerve.

....

16.

....

Breakdance Lecture cont'd: We hope they don't become serial killers because no one ever called them "sugarlips." But then who are "we"? Who are "we" to speak of "they"? What about Marty's uncle and Martin Heidegger? (Of course time itself manifests itself as the horizon of Being! Who ever thought otherwise.) What ever became of "them"? Did "they" ever feel "they" had to put "I" in quotes? Was being more simple then than time? I don't know, maybe this line of thought leads to the same place game roosters go when the game's over or when the curate says I now pronounce you Man and Babe without quotes and quotes someone else's pronouns at length out of Bartlett or the Bible to beef up the occasion. "Who would succeed in the world should be wise in the use of his (sic) pronouns." John Milton Hay, 1838-1905 Or Gertrude Stein saying pronouns are not really the name of anything. "They represent some one but they are not its or his (sic) name."

....

17.

....

Breakdance Lecture cont'd: Then as now a woman could be stoned to
death for defending her brother or dishonoring her father. Now, in more
civilized societies, a man can be murdered in a dispute over his place in the
popcorn line at the local cinema and every woman he ever knew or loved is
protected by law. Of course, many people in Japan have been killed by
falling TVs during earthquakes. Mother Nature has adapted her wiley
ways. Or a woman jumps out of a moving cab on the FDR parkway
without leaving a note or any other indication. In an entirely predictable
coincidence, every speaker at the symposium began with a quote from
Wittgenstein who tried his best during his complicated and lonely life to
confess his sins to all he had offended.

....

so great was her de   sire to learn the truth

of Zen   whose his   tory is a function

precisely of this no   longer startling idea

of the giving up of   all vain pride to silence

FIG.17

18.

With or without sooner or later developments of Huang Po or some other
sagacious Po little dogs will be named after in the modern era / griffins
used as furniture legs in Asia Minor c. 800 BC/E / as for question of
whether or not women in the modern era should shave their legs it's much
more complicated than anyone would have ever dreamed / 800 BC/E not
yet possible to have full   experience of
gravity or to see certain th   ings in certain
lights / although suburbs fou   nd in ancient
Greece / fabric dyes made fro   m purple snails
SOON we'll play golf on t   he moon! he
exclaimed / museum   guard sketching
collection from Car   FIG.18   thage that con
tains urns with sacrificed children stuffed inside / evolutionary time: not
known when bees began seeing landing strips on flowers / post and lintel
just as basic in Greek architecture as apex of right triangle obtending
toward flower / the word jasmine (*gelsemium sempervirens*) approaches
flower with greater semantic volocity than its Latin predecessor / will the
academic ever lie in a meadow thinking only of her lucky nose /

19.

My Chinese guest moved in with a 50lb bag of rice & fished for carp in the nearby canal / in reality there is nothing to be grasped / warned wailed / even if wanted to / atomic clocks buried all around the naval observatory / til the end of time, as they say / if language is as notoriously intransitive as they say we may have to design more verb constructions that don't need objects to complete their meaning / in every new era there's so much to be done! / disguised as the guy with the weird name he / yes, that wretched Archduke was a maniacal hunter who killed 6,000 stags in his lifetime, 2,763 seagulls in one day / Rousseau denied an original tension with the state of nature / tough sea-going gear and eyes that search beyond their own reflection serve her well / condemned to study the Clapper Rail without ever having seen one / murmuring awestruck blinded with pain / J.J. Pickle defends his fellow Texan down to the wire / yes, intellectual and political life indistinguisable in Confucianism but did that really make things better or worse / before long Hadrian will have had the opportunity to build a concrete dome so large and beautiful 5th century barbarians will be too awed to sack the Pantheon / or so the story goes /

20.

Noticed disturbing grammatical constructions among speakers engaged in
breeding faster greyhounds / MEANWHILE: 1794 CE, an Iroquois courier
named Sharp Shins runs 90 miles across the hills of western New York in
less time than it takes a classical tragedy to unfold at a rate faster than it
took Roger Bannister to run the first 4 minute mile / a blue ribbon team
will be developing more broadly applicable definitions of death / in
October 1989 she was quoted as saying, this coup in Panama was unusual
in its violence, these days most things happen on the phone / (hi, let's talk
about this, ok? zap whomp gulp, you speak the Esperanto?) / the better
part of several hundred years might well have been devoted to depicting
and redepicting centaurs tormented by lust / myths of desperate adults
become fairytales of curious tots / water now up to second floor just as s/he
learns the greatest pre-Islamic poet c. 600 CE may have been a woman:
al-Khansã' replied, "I wear a sidãr because I was not aware of its prohibition"
/ water now up to roof / al-Khansã' wrote, *walking slowly and seeming to
bend forward every time I [try to] stand up [straight]* /

21.

....

<u>Breakdance Lecture</u> cont'd: The truth is "I" want to wear funny shoes and juggle while balancing a glass of water on "my" head, but "I" am not sure of the identity or the mechanics of <u>that</u> "I." This would be an act beyond grammar "I" suspect, like any referent in a life or death situation in which I don't believe what you're telling me so what am I to do? (As fear mounts, quotation marks drop like flies.) None of this is my language, actually. Just my arrangement of it and maybe that solves the problem of I think therefore who the fuck do you think you are. The pronouns we inhabit for a while and then pass on to others. Treat them well. Stewards all. And yet I do at times feel frighteningly like a proper noun. Maybe that's the problem. The 'I don't want to not appear self-effacing but' routine don't get no one no where no how. This is agony, agonistic, agonizing, but fun. *For word of wynd, lityl trespase* [Digby 102, c. 1410]

....

22.

al-Khansā' wrote, *But for the multitude of people round me weeping for their [world] I would have killed myself* / more recently a journalist's Dalmatian licks up blood on the floor of the bar at the Hotel Commodore on a page in the book *From Beirut to Jerusalem* / there is many a real-life thriller at the center of gravity of one Archimedean magnitude subtracted from another, "the same point is the center of gravity of the remaining portion if the same point was the center of gravity both of the whole and of the part removed" / (I sincerely hope knowing this will help. JR) / the eternal meanwhile in Jerusalem goes on and on as the foreign press drains one glass after another / elsewhere "dashikis & brightly colored batik skirts costumed the locals as they prayed" / it's a socio-geometrical truth that only the initiated can know / centers remain, you know, long after their environs have been removed / upstream reaches once rich in caribou, musk oxen, fox, seal, and fish are now depleted / in the close-up one can discern jest jealousy jump-rope jello-mold justice jetliners jocks jokes jabberwocky jeers Jesus Jeanne d'Arc Jeeves ..... / please remain calm, we are here to see you through the fastmoving J series /

23.

We've come this far only to find there are things no genre can contain /
Plotinus (c. 205-270) thought jest a form of contemplation / 1200 CE
cathedrals collapsing all over Europe / late 20th century CE they came to
count on instant replay and lost touch with the urgency of attention /
Hadrian's head c. 100 CE already seems destined to be replaced by
Constantine's in the frieze / date please: arguments from authority
collapsing all over Europe / in Homer, the young scholar argued, there is
no notion of absolute impossibility: some feats beyond destiny seem to
work / Chartres will burn and be rebuilt 4 times long after Thales (elemental
moisture) Zeno (laws against motion) Parmenides (nothing can be named
that isn't real) Heraclitus (mortals are immortals and vice versa, the one
living the other's death and dying the other's life) / much later flying
buttresses seen as material proof of God's existence / thing is is it's almost
over soon as it's begun, right? / Hobbes will warn—too late?—against
leniency toward grandees / Pascal will die at 39 never knowing outcome of
his wager /

24.

....

Breakdance Lecture cont'd: Thing is that all these characters may have
made each other up and where does that leave me, or you, or them— that
is, us? Why do I always try to see geometry in nature, she asked abruptly,
obviously in great pain. Philosophers have perhaps spent too much time
discussing pain, wrote J.L. Austin. (Criterion # 1 for irreversible coma:
unreceptivity and unresponsibility even to intensely painful stimuli.
Harvard Ad Hoc Committee, 1968.)

....

900 BC/E geometric designs appear in Greek art / rationalism still on the
rise in China squelching mysticism of Shang (Yin) dynas
                    ty. Greeks have not yet solved problem of hu
            man figure — HOW TO: stay inside the lines and
        still make it look real / that's OK one day Du
    champ awoke & knew a ready-made could be correct
        ed, assisted, rectified, signed! / here! — almost wrote hear—
    silent turn to listen circa now / look s/he exclaimed & FIG.24
    appeared / then listen / hear the not quite but almost allegorical
    sea / civilization is the rationalization of what we can't help doing (art
    says Johns says Cage, is a series of helpless acts) / look, no worry,
        whatever else it'll always be circa now and then /

25.
Let's try to get it right this time the teacher says: step step slide step step
step shuffle slide kick / women interviewed about what it's like to lead a
life in today's world with hairy legs say the problem of how to get the
human figure right in art & life seems now always to have been just another
gender recursive politically inscribed structural trap in which one is
coerced to wear uncomfortable clothing, particularly shoes / which piece
of information to put where—never a benign puzzle—has become an
emergency / here's the song you need to learn before history moves on / c.
yesterday, today, tomorrow Congolese Sri Lankans stateless Jews
Palestinians South & North Koreans stateless Palestinians South & North
Vietnamese Somalis Sudanese Ugandans Rawandans Bosnians Serbs
Croations Muslim Indians Pakistanis Iraquis Afgans and so many more flee
wander take refuge watch their lives crumble into dust / c. 800 BC/E
Carthaginians on the rise economically / headline (1999) RELICS OF
CARTHAGE SHOW BRUTALITY AMID GOOD LIFE / African slave
trade thriving in thriving markets across thriving Europe and the thriving
Americas / singing Celts arrive in Britain c. 600 BC/E / it's important to
learn how to read faster write a business letter make a speech write a
résumé / otherwise it's Moby Dick all over again minus the whale / *mene,
mene, tekel, upharsin,* usually translated "thou art weighed in the balance
and found wanting" /

26.

....

Breakdance Lecture cont'd with guest appearances: In the interest of
semiotics they walked to the end of the hall and came to a room with two
windows. He threw his tie over his shoulder. It didn't fall to the floor. First
test successfully passed: knot holds. He— another "he"—looked up to
inquire, Any specific topic? Traffic roared below the open windows. The
noise could have masked the sound of the third man approaching. Life in
the fast lane, said the one with the necktie, and snickered. It seemed an
unremarkable remark in an unremarkable scene, at the time, an unremarkable
scene during the kind of unremarkable day that breeds addictions. This is in
fact the kind of scene in which one suspects
something terrible
is about to happen.
Otherwise why take such
pains to notice it? (Or, why   FIG.26   would the writer
take such pains to describe it?) What would it mean *in medias res* to
consider all this a sufficient example of the making of meaning? The man
with the tie looks into the eyes of the other, the one who wanted to know
the topic. The man with the tie opens his mouth wide to yawn, or perhaps
to answer. Perhaps he was about to say something smart or perhaps afterall
he was about to yawn. This is the moment we all instantly recognize—at
one and the same time a bodily and linguistic precipice. A shot might ring
out or not as the case may be. The topic could be murder. But the first man
shifts his gaze beyond the other toward a long view out the window. There,
in a park across the street, he sees Francis Bacon standing in the snow,
leaving us to speculate on genre.

....

27.

I do a lot of channel surfing she admits / her dream is to spend two months in the south of France / or maybe in Vienna thinking about Wittgenstein's confessions or Freud's potboilers or the comic antics of the Vienna Circle, laced with the Logical Positivist scandal, etc – each thought will come while eating a differet torte in a different Viennese café / Possible Explanation: As a child she may have seen the installment of Sesame Street when Cookie Monster discovers the moon is not a cookie / meanwhile more frantic goings on: hatred of hair, straightening of hair, siege on body odors by means of strongly scented deodorants, pads, aftershaves, soaps, gels, sprays, candy colored mouthwashes, concealing creams, starving, vomiting, nose jobs & other plastic surgeries / *the sun went down and all the lanes grew dark* / later they all learn all about catharsis, natural law, zeitgeist, enlightenment, irony, & difference as post-modern term / it's really fun being part of Western Civ / though it's already been a long time since an ordinary citizen in Italy discussed his health in elegiac verse /

28.

Does fractal geometry really apply to history? / why not! / who can deny
the many replicating breaks, the many changes of scale / the tumescent and
turbulent developments over time / and though the exegetes generally

agree that bees actually do see

runways on flowers / books over

due at library / garbage ne

eds to go out / Troy excav

ations reveal city descr

ibed in Iliad at sixth l

evel / and every year anoth

er 10,000 decimal po

ints are added to pi / and yo

u've worked hard to make your lawn and garden beautiful but the only
things coming up are those dirt mounds that announce you've got gophers!
/ hard not to feel demoralized but try / THAT WHICH IS light warm rare
fire is male / THAT WHICH IS dark cold heavy dense is female / surely
you jest /

FIG.28

29.

back to 800 BC/E (really hard to move on isn't it) when stories told by the
Homers already old / any 16th or 18th or 20th (to skip the odds) century
mind could be mounted on a strangely detached tripod of time and gain
unique perspective / ah yes, yes, exactly when and where did time become
space? / women told to eat one Brazil nut a day for sufficient dietary sele-
nium / c. 1990 CE an elderly neighbor pets my dog and says, It's too bad;
we're really stuck; this is not one of your better centuries, you know. /

....

Breakdance Lecture cont'd: I don't want to believe any of this of course.
You understand the of course I believe. Between believing and doubt what
else is there to play with once we've got our pronouns straight or at least
are able to use them with straight faces. Will any of this, for instance, help
us through Kierkegaard's three stages of 'live and learn'? I.E. From the
aesthetic to the ethical to the religious? Is that even where I want to go now
that I've got my I back?

....

30.

THREE RING CIRCA CONT'D

The fanciful species will always find ways to get by or so they think / c.
600 BC/E Assyrian soldiers use animal bladders as water wings to swim
across selected bodies of water and make sneak attacks / throughout the
Lebanese Civil War an elderly Englishman showed up at the Beirut
Country Club every day to play a solitary game of golf / You say "finally"
only to make the next moment pass its gases with merciful speed!, she
screamed at her bewildered husband / tipping ferries have been drowning
thousands every year for years / this is not a metaphysical or metaphorical
or geopolitical observation / turn a page (physical activity good for the
health) space becomes time / try your best to distinguish between pre &
post-prandial theories of pre & postmodern eras and check the appropriate
box / c. 1000 CE Avicenna's improvement over Aristotle: prophesy is to
know the middle term without having to study logic /

31.

Look, even though it's c. 2000 AD / we should still all be praying all the
time for deliverence from error, said a representative of a major world religion
as he jiggled the coffee urn during the break at the conference / 1278 CE
invention of glass mirrors sends thousands into irremediable shock / every
event can be an occasion to notice god / why would anyone try to make
anything appear real in art [s/he asked, scratching a fresh mosquito bite] /
Excuse me don't those brackets belong to Merleau-Ponty? And whose
hyphen was that! I protest! / c. 800 BC/E it's déjà vu all over it's all over
again: Egyptians write fable called "Battle between Head and Belly" that
just about says it all is all I have to say / c. 500 BC/E Heraclitus says it all
many times over thereby seeming to contradict one of the "it"s he's said
just prior / no problem, nema problema, kein problem, geen probleem,
nessun problema / an infinity of "it"s saves the day everyday things are
getting better & better, QED / all of the preceding has been scribbled in a
margin of late vacated by various Fermats with their famous excuses / as
long as the words come in the singing everything will be ok /

32.

Before anyone could compile all the useful substitutes for "said" s/he had already supposed, thought, whispered, alleged, held, boasted, bleated, snorted, shouted, believed, hinted, elaborated, grunted, answered, explained, retorted, fumed, replied, mumbled, claimed, yearned, barked, fumed, cursed, debated, ejaculated, giggled, spelled out, hissed, allowed, averred, argued, blurted, pleaded, lied, insisted, sworn, proposed, implied, insinuated, gloated, urged, inviegled, suggested, promised, screamed, taunted, screeched, bellowed, begged, spat out, resumed /

....

Breakdance Lecture cont'd: Right now I want another edge to open up on this page. I want it to be thrilling. I want it to be frightening. I want to be startled awake by its suddenness. I want it more than I can say.

....

So what if Syrian language changes from Phoenician to Aramaic / woman reigns as high priest in Thebes / Aristotelian logic is based on Gk grammar; Arabic logic on Arabic / problems of incommensurables not easy to solve / bombs go off in hotels, markets and cafés on sunny days / authors of childrens' lit reject tragedy in favor of horror /

33.

....

Breakdance Lecture cont'd: This act of writing is a physical act, an act of
my body not yet fully in contact with my mind. In fact at times it seems my
body has a mind of its own. It stretches out in some completely surprising,
frivolous motion. It's understood that "frivolous motion" is a legal term. I
think I'm beginning to understand some but not all of the implications. I
know the body-mind problem is out of date, along with the problem of evil,
but I can't help thinking this way.

....

[   ] Sardis [   ]

] often she turns her thoughts to this place....

[the rest of this poem is in tatters]

N PLUS ZERO

Why use procedures when one can simply note the succession of things that "naturally" come to mind? "Act so that there is no use in a centre," said Gertrude Stein. Good advice, particularly if the center is "self" without the benefit of centrifugal artifice.

(**Procedure** : instructions for how to go on : what Beckett didn't give Didi and Gogo; what Wittgenstein gave himself in the *Tractatus* (numerical momentum), etc.)

Strange concept, self; not strange enough. Hence, the "natural" fallacy. Procedural artifice is a form of authorial agency which nonetheless brings a tonic otherness to a composition: deflecting single point perspective, opening the field to dialogic alterity, alter-texts, if not egos, in equally disadvantaged conversation. Hence the necessity of humor.

The question is whether such devices are useful for our self-absorbed species, accumulating endless wants and highly evolved needs in what seems to be a geometric progression of consumption-targeted quests for increasingly improbable satisfaction whose most cherished image is found in the mirror. A literature of reciprocal alterity, if such a thing is possible, can't fix this culture-wide entanglement with short-sighted narcissism, but it may present significantly alternative sites for making meaning.

Methodical interrogations of authorial identity can induce vertigo (if not nausea) in those not mechanically inclined. Most Oulipean models to-date have been resolutely mechanical, not willingly subject to the 2nd law of thermodynamics with its steamy entropic irreversibility. This can give the illusion that nothing dire is at stake. (It's a game.) In principle, one can always rewind the clock to tick backwards restoring any spacio-temporal starting point. The mechanics of Oulipean procedures may differ radically from chance or ecologically modeled operations that make wagers with chaos. At the same time, the futility of any procedures designed to bypass recognitions of uncertainty, despair, radical doubt, imbues them with an elegiac strain.

Procedures that embody methodical doubt along with structural optimism can become interrogatively driven heat-seeking devices that zero in on the manifest unintelligibility of our complex material predicament. This takes place in the zone between the familiar and the terrifyingly unknown. That in-between zone is for me the location of the most interesting cultural work.

The Humor of the Procedural Elegiac is lodged in its attempt at playful escape from self-serving gestures while never fully eluding strategies of desire. The grave and ludic performance of committed alterity is an inherently perverse enterprise in its off-centering of our happy narcissism. Here comes, not everybody, but the necessary illusion of other logically possible selves and worlds, other ness monsters vigorously invading, cavorting in what may have formerly been one's (note apostrophic claim) poem.

Poetics is an extreme noticing of how language works in the illuminated space-time brackets of a composition. Hence, N plus Zero equals A to Z in what remains of this essay, with N standing, not for "noun," but for "next" and zero for a certain degree of cluelessness; i.e., the familiar quandary, what to do next?

Begin now to notice with sensual precision. Nothing is as it seems, nor is it otherwise. A narrative sets out, a succession of one thing after another. Literary Procedures like procedural memories keep us on track via a succession of presents that, counter to some avant-garde claims, are logically, neurologically prohibited from presenting the future. The future is an ever shifting hypothetical and, as Lucretius might have put it, it most interestingly resides in the inclination of neurons to swerve a little from their course.

For a long time there has been the interesting idea—Aristotelian, La Fontainean—that to achieve an ethical life one (any one, of any species) has to act against/outside one's own nature. Apart from that troublesome term "nature," the chief conundrum may be that if we go resolutely from

A to Z

A poem that begins in history perhaps because it was too sparsely perhaps because it was too sparsely adorned because much has disappeared or is no longer apparent and what we became the surface became seemed seemed

then not to have been there from the first from the first very confused about
this but and sorting through one inkling after another after made the luxury
packaging made it all bearable all the disasters disasters and their probable
etiologies now no longer viewed in cinema newsreels while eating while
eating pop corn and candy and rattling ice in large paper cups of here on
this planet moved we have all moved on to assorted TVs and now their
aftermath is all there is to some who think that all this I think this is I think
this or that because the pain or any experience of pain first hand or through
the transmission that causes could compassion or empathy could turn out to
be as humorous as other alternatives from someone else's point of view just
as the voice the voiceover voice says let's make a pact that will help us
learn from our mistakes or the mistakes of others others impinge upon our
lives compulsory happiness is a spur of a sort of spur to buck up and deny
how bad it all is not wanting to be alone in one's condition e.g. utopia love
it or leave it as alone alone they set out and or zig hoping for evolutionary
characteristics or gardens to kick in evolutionary characteristics that may
generate caring responses or wanting to state before going any further to
say the literal sense of the figurative as it awakens neurons to shoot the
moon at many many synapses poets are are not most importantly profli-
gates or fools or purveyors of wisdom so then what the hell are they hey
about that poem what noises did it make what exactly did it look like and
what happened at the end at the end they're all just quoting the dictionary
yes I know just when did tourism replace pilgrimage and or has it and or
were they always the same in the face of what so much predatory intention
love of reason what if sublimation does induce melancholia x-y out each
word is a stroke of genius that could bring on all the rest

A poem that begins in history perhaps because it was too sparsely perhaps
because it was   Very us that sparsely rattling quoting poem or no much
longer kick just in to achieve an ethical life one (any one, of any species)
has to act against/outside one's   History gardens from etiologies
disasters confused begins a was was what we were nature   Apart from
questions of defining "nature," the chief conundrum may be that if
While while we who will wanting zig wanting wisdom what what
what   What yes   One believes in laws of that egregiously
indefinable term, then acting outside one's   When were what x-y
word too sparsely adorned because much has disappeared   To be
able to act outside one's nature is one's nature   Inside out outside
in   Was very us that sparsely rattling quoting poem or no much

longer kick just in   How to manage your gadgets how to prepare
for death or life   How to find solace in language with all its
anarchic referents or   History gardens from etiologies disasters
confused begins a zig yes x-y   The pensive edges into melancholy
without constraints to spur us on to play   X-y was very us that
sparsely rattling quoting poem or no much longer kick just in   We
are not designed to perceive most of what surrounds us or to fully
understand the rest   History gardens from etiologies disasters
confused begins a zig yes   The celebration of the combinatorial
excess with these 5 integers with this fractal curve the escape from
finitude begins   Yes x-y was very us that sparsely rattling quoting
poem or no much longer kick   The manic combinatorics of the fugue
inducing giddy ecstasy in the listener   Just in history gardens from
etiologies disasters   Confused begins a zig it's the nature of music to
elude questions of fallibility the poetic claim to zig   Yes x-y was
very us that sparsely rattling quoting poem or no much longer kick
Flotillas of swallowtails disappear into themselves   This is neither
true nor false in history gardens from etiologies   Confused
begins again from A to Z   In the face of so much predatory
intention   Love of reason   What if sublimation does induce
melancholia   Each word is a stroke of genius that could bring on
all the rest

PROCEDURAL & SOURCE NOTES

<u>Procedure. Elegy. Humor</u>. Illuminated with help from the OED.

<u>word ends...</u>. language taken from: Maurice Sendak's, *Higglety, Pigglety, Pop*; Jürgen Habermas's, *Knowledge and Human Interests*; Michel Foucault's *The Order of Things*; Rainer Maria Rilke's First Duino Elegy; Gertrude Stein's *Stanzas in Meditation*.

<u>Existence Is An Attribute</u> The epigraph is from Immanuel Kant, *Critique of Pure Reason,* Second Division: Transcendental Dialectic, Book II, Chapter III, Section 4. "The Impossibility of an Ontological Proof of the Esistence of God." (Trans. Norman Kemp Smith. New York: St. Martin's Press, 1965. p.500 ff.)

<u>Earth Heaven and Hell</u>
Names of magazines are from a subscription form attached to "College Ruled" spiral bound notebooks in the early1980s.

<u>Oh Mother Goose Oh Yin Oh Yang</u>
Epigraphs, postlogue and parenthetical descriptions of violence from *The Annotated Mother Goose*, New York: Clarkson N. Potter, 1962.

<u>A I D /I/ S A P P E A R A N C E</u>
The disappearance moves through the letters of the alphabet (and the source text) in this way: Beginning with letters A I D S, it spreads to adjoining letters B H J C E R T, to F G K Q U, to L P V, to M O W, to N X, to Y.
    Part of text in the first stanza is from "The Atomic Theory and the Fundamental Principles underlying the Description of Nature" in *The Philosophical Writings of Niels Bohr, Volume 1, Atomic Theory and the Description of Nature*. Woodbridge, Connecticut, 1987.

<u>THE BLUE STARES</u>
Barbara Guest's "The Blue Stairs" is the title poem in her 1968 volume *The Blue Stairs* (Corinth Books). I have used most of her words (italicized) in the original order. The procedure I used interspersed my own language from a notebook I carried with me to Budapest, The Czech Republic, and Vancouver, B.C., Fall 1996, and finally to Berkeley where I visited Guest. The number of letters and words in the title determined numerical factors in the composition of the poem. The epigraph and several other phrases are from Julia Kristeva's essay "Giotto's Joy," *Desire in Language* (Columbia, 1980). All Italian words are from Dante's *Inferno*. I decided to "write on" Guest's poem when I discovered that it was not reprinted in her 1995 selected poems and was therefore unavailable to readers.

<u>NOT A CAGE</u>
This poem is composed from beginnings and endings of books I was culling from my library in the Fall of 1990.

Steinzas in Mediation
Numerals I-XV are followed by the first words of lines in the corresponding sections of Part I of Gertrude Stein's *Stanzas in Meditation*.

WITT & STEIN
Written for Jackson Mac Low's 80th Birthday. Epigraphic quotes from Wittgenstein are respectively from *Tractatus* 2.012, 6.4, 6.41. All Stein quotes are from *How to Write* (Sun & Moon, 1995, 141). All language in italics is from Jackson Mac Low's "Unannounced Slights" (Forties 1), in *Thing of Beauty: New and Selected Works*. Berkeley, University of California Press, 2008.

Archimedes' New Light
This poem includes language from *Geometrical Solutions Derived From Mechanics: A Treatise of Archimedes, Recently Discovered And Translated From The Greek By Dr. J.L. Heiberg, Professor of Classical Philology At The University of Copenhagen*. La Salle Illinois: The Open Court Publishing Company, 1942, (Copyright 1909). The subtitle is derived from Alan Devenish's "Geometry of the Excitable Species."

Coimbra Poem of Poetry & Violence: Grief's Rubies
During the VI Encontro Internacional De Poetas, 24 a 27 de Maio de 2007, Universidade de Coimbra, Portugal, Forrest Gander and I discovered that we were both "writing through" the readings that all participants were attending. They were occuring in over a dozen languages. The Meetings were on Poetry and Violence, and also in honor of the 250th anniversary of the birth of William Blake. After we noticed and discussed what we were each doing, we decided to collaborate on a dialogic composition of our responses to the polylingual presentations at Coimbra. Margin to margin entries are Gander's.

/ WESTERN CIV CONT'D /
For many of the circas in this poem, I am indebted to *The Timetable of History: A Horizontal Linkage of People and Events*. By Bernard Grun, based upon Werner Stein's *Kulturfahrplan: Who Did What Concurrently Through the Ages of Man...* New York: Simon and Schuster, 1982. My gratitude to Marty Gearhart and apologies to many authors and publishers over the fullness of time for driveby unattributed use. The majority of the language in the poem can be blamed on noone but me.

N PLUS ZERO was originally written for the Newlipo panel at the 2008 AWP meetings and revised for publication in ecopoetics no. 6/7.

PLUS A to Z
Originally a 26 page poem written for Tom & Val Raworth. Each page underwent removal of words beginning with successive letters of the alphabet. The poem has since undergone many other realizations in live performances that always begin with the original first—A—page. The version in this volume, at the end of the concluding essay, is the result of a new set of permutative improvisations.

ROOF BOOKS

the best in language since 1976

Recent & Selected Titles

Roof Books are distributed by
SMALL PRESS DISTRIBUTION
1341 Seventh Street • Berkeley, CA. 94710-1403.
spdbooks.org

Roof Books are published by
Segue Foundation
300 Bowery #2 • New York, NY 10012
seguefoundation.com